Following Jesus
Into the Power

Jerry Daley

with Jerome Daley

Game On Coaching
219 Mossy Spring Lane
Boone NC 28607

www.gameoncoach.com

© 2015 by Jerry Daley

Scripture quotations, unless otherwise noted, are taken from the New American Standard Bible®, copyright © 1960, 1962, 1963, 1968, 1971, 1972, 1973, 1975, 1977, 1995 by The Lockman Foundation. Used by permission. (www.Lockman.org)

Cover design: Jerome Daley

Images: Dreamstime.com

Interior layout: Jerome Daley

ISBN-13: 978-1514195383

ISBN-10: 1514195380

CONTENTS

FORWARD

Following Jesus into the Power is an invitation into the life of the Holy Spirit so that Jesus may maximize His Glory within us. Jerry points out that people who love God deeply often see God's service as a matter of right believing, right behaving, and right speaking rather than demonstrating the kingdom power of Jesus.

We often see miracles as something unique, something that is beyond ourselves. Having walked with Jerry for seven years, I know he believes and lives the conviction that Jesus' power is available every day of the year to every person who is surrendered to Jesus. This book explains why and how miracles should be a part of our everyday lives and not for special people at special times.

He simply and clearly states what our lives must look like in order for the kingdom of God to continue to advance today, both inside us and through us to touch others. I love Jerry and I am thrilled he's getting some of his thoughts and life on paper. We cannot afford to miss the lessons in this valuable book.

~ Patrick Lai, founder OPEN Network and author of *Tentmaking* and *Business for Transformation*

INTRODUCTION

I was standing in front of about fifteen college students, circled tightly on random couches and chairs in the small dormitory living room. "When Jesus did His miracles on earth, was He operating as God or operating as man?" As my question hung in the air, a sense of electric possibility rose. A thoughtful silence lingered as people's faces registered concentration.

"I think His miracles were more of a God-thing," one young lady volunteered. "A sign that the kingdom of God was drawing near in a brand new way." Several heads nodded.

"I don't know," spoke up another. "We know that Jesus was both fully divine and fully human, so why wouldn't His miracles be a demonstration of what God can do through a totally-yielded human?"

"I like the idea of that," said the first one, "but I haven't raised anyone from the dead lately." A chuckle rolled across the room accompanied by wistful smiles.

"That said," she continued, "I did have the coolest experience yesterday! I was standing in line at the grocery store behind a young mother with two kids on a sugar high. One was grabbing magazines off the rack while the other was groaning and complaining about his tummy hurting. I felt an intense compassion for all of them, especially the boy holding his stomach, and I impulsively leaned over and asked the mom if I could pray for her son. She was glazed over but said yes.

"As I took the little boy's hands and asked Jesus to heal him, both of the children quieted down remarkably. I guess they were surprised that a stranger was talking to God about them! But as the little boy relaxed, his mom teared up and thanked me kindly. She even went on to talk about what a tough day they'd had and how she'd lost her babysitter last minute. I told her I could probably do some babysitting on the weekends if she still needed help.

"The whole encounter was over in about a minute, but the presence of God felt really strong to me. I don't know if you'd call that a miracle, but I did feel the Holy Spirit in an unusual way. It felt really good."

"Jenna," I said, "You've just preached my message for me! And I'll have to go with answer B: that Jesus lived and ministered in the supernatural out of His humanity, not His divinity…and I'll tell more about why that is in a few minutes. But let's look at the fork in the road prompted by this question; the answer we give here will take us in very different directions."

And so it did! As we explored this powerful idea together as a group, the two paths took on a striking clarity. To the extent that Christians see miracles as something that God does through a unique, once-in-the-history-of-the-world Savior, to that extent the supernatural is the domain of the Other. It's the God-realm, far removed from our role as mere mortals in the service of God. We read the stories of Jesus and are led to adoration and worship. Which is good, of course, but it's not the whole story.

To the extent that we see Jesus' miracles as something that God does through surrendered, anointed humans, whoa... That takes us somewhere radically different! That makes Jesus the first Christian, the example and model of what our lives can look like. What our lives *must* look like in order for the kingdom of God to continue to advance today. This is the source of our power as followers and ambassadors of Christ, and power is what we need to live out our calling in this world.

Plugging into the Power

Power was a crucial topic to the risen Jesus, who gave strict instructions to His growing community of followers to not leave Jerusalem—in other words, to not even think about stepping into the Great Commission—until the Holy Spirit was poured out on them! So the "Acts" of the apostles didn't kick into gear until that divine anointing came in the form of fire resting on their heads…and when that happened, the supernatural started to break out everywhere. Every person present became dangerous!

Just like Jenna was dangerous standing in line at the grocery store. The Holy Spirit in her picked up on the needs in that young family and activated divine compassion and boldness. Was it a miracle, a healing? Probably. Was it supernatural? Absolutely! And the result was kingdom impact.

What if all of God's people were on constant alert for these kinds of God-moments?

What if we expected God to prompt us to people's needs…and then empower us with the exact answer to those needs, whether it be a prayer for healing, a physical act of kindness, or a divine revelation? What if we entered into each day with the joy of the hunt—the search for someone to love on? I'll tell you what would happen: the kingdom of God would show up in radical ways!

And this is precisely what Jesus came to do, to equip us to be an extension of His supernatural love in the world. To be who He was and to do what He did. We don't have to "be God" in the same way Jesus was because the power of God resides in us by the Holy Spirit, and because of that, we are the representatives of

Christ across this world today. This short book is an invitation into the life of the Spirit so that we can continue the works of Jesus.

"Truly, truly, I say to you, he who believes in Me, the works that I do, he will do also; and greater works than these he will do; because I go to the Father" (John 14:12). In the following chapters, let's take a closer look at what Jesus had in mind.

1. FUELED UP!

Following Jesus into Holy Spirit Dependency

The words never fail to move me deeply: "You are My beloved Son, in You I am well-pleased." Jesus has just started His public ministry, and He really hasn't done anything of substance yet. But the Father is well-pleased with Him! Not pleased with *what He has done* but pleased with *who He is*. Just as the Father is pleased with us His children, not for what we have done or what we will do one day but simply for who we are. Daughters and sons, every one of us.

This proclamation from God comes audibly from the heavens as John the Baptist dips Jesus beneath the waters of the Jordan River in a prophetic act of baptism. The Holy Spirit descends on Jesus in the form of a dove and "remains" on Him (John 1:33). This might prompt two questions: 1) if Jesus was a sinless human, why did He need to be baptized? and 2) if Jesus was divine, why did He need to receive the Spirit?

Jesus Himself answered the first question by saying that it was to "fulfill all righteousness" (Matthew 3:15), alluding to this as an inauguration rather than a cleansing. In the Old Testament it was customary for any newly-appointed prophet, priest, or king to be anointed with oil as a sign of the Spirit of God. This act was an official recognition of the office bestowed. For Jesus (as a combination of prophet, priest, and king) this act was His formal anointing and commissioning into active ministry.

It's worth noting that Jesus' baptism was not regeneration—not the inner shift from spiritual death to spiritual life that each of us experiences at a providential moment in time. His divine origin and nature meant that He entered the world spiritually alive from day one, even as an infant. Jesus didn't have to "get saved," but He did have to be anointed.

So what about the second question? If Jesus was already fully divine, why did He need to "receive" the Holy Spirit? This question leads us closer to the message of this book: Jesus, because He laid aside His divine characteristics by becoming a man, needed the infilling of the Holy Spirit just as we do. He would be the "prototype Christian"—the *first* Christian if you will—who related to the Father, to His world, and to His calling by way of the third Person of the Trinity.

The Humanity of Jesus

This is an important point, so let's review that again. By assuming humanity, Jesus voluntarily laid aside, not His divine nature but the divine "benefits" we might call them. Think here about the "omni" attributes of God: omnipotence (all power), omniscience (all knowing), omnipresence (everywhere present), etc. These qualities were His by right and by nature, but He elected to participate in the human condition so fully, so completely, that He stripped Himself temporarily of these divine benefits.

Paul says in Philippians 2:6-7 that Jesus "did not regard equality with God a thing to be grasped, but emptied Himself, taking the form of a servant and being made in the likeness of men." This *emptying* put His earthly journey squarely in our shoes. Hebrews describes how this emptying was necessary in order for Jesus to enter fully into the human experience: "For we do not have a high priest who cannot sympathize with our weaknesses, but One who has been tempted in all things as we are, yet without sin" (Hebrews 4:15). *He* became *us*!

In other words, Jesus lived His days functionally on planet earth as a sinless human, not a divine messenger. If it were just a message that humans needed, God could have sent an angel; instead, this kingdom invasion and race redemption called for a much more dramatic (and costly) mission: God become man.

Jesus emphasized His humanity by constantly referring to Himself as the "Son of Man"—twenty eight times in the book of Matthew alone. It's not until the very end of the road, right before His crucifixion that Jesus references Himself as "Son of God." He seems to want the disciples to understand as clearly as possible that He is living in the same humanity they know so well.

Immanuel was Isaiah's prophetic term for Jesus, describing Him as "God with us." This radical "with-ness" required a fully human condition. Jesus became the God who did not merely approach us…or the God who sent a message to us…or even the God who let us off the hook. Jesus *became* us! He took on a body and emotions and an autonomous will and participated 100% in the experience of being human. It is a profound level of identification that goes the whole distance.

And the impact of this divine experiment was unprecedented. For the first time ever, men and women had a chance to see what it looks like for Someone to live fully in the kingdom of God, to be completely surrendered to the Father's initiative, and to move in the power of the Spirit as He did the Father's will.

A Wake-up Call

How has the church of Jesus missed making this a priority for so long? Across much of the Body of Christ we have people who love God deeply and align themselves with the church community but who see the kingdom call as a matter of right believing, right behaving, and right speaking (sharing their testimony)...rather than demonstrating the kingdom power Jesus evidenced.

But this was the reason Jesus commanded His newly-formed church community to do nothing—*nothing!*—until clothed with the power of the Holy Spirit, which in turn anointed them with supernatural power. Power to love, power to see others, and even power to do miraculous things. Things continuing today all over the world. And this is precisely what the world needs: the actions of God, not just the words. The word of God with skin on.

Listen to Paul's testimony in 1 Corinthians 2:4-5, where he declares that "my message and my preaching were not in persuasive words of wisdom, but in demonstration of the Spirit and of power, *that your faith should not rest on the wisdom of men, but on the power of God.*" Apparently, God intends to see more of the Christ-life flowing through His children than we ever thought possible!

And it doesn't have to be overly sensational. Just ask Jenna. As the saying goes, *Small things done with great love will change the world.* There is a power in being led by the Spirit that doesn't necessarily draw attention to ourselves. The more we learn to pay attention to the Spirit, the more it shows up in *supernaturally natural* ways. In a little while we'll look more closely at the gifts of the Spirit and how they work in our lives, but first let's look at how they operated in Jesus' life.

The Yieldedness of Jesus

Jesus shared His secret with us in John 5:19, "Truly, truly, I say to you, the Son can do nothing of Himself, unless it is something He sees the Father doing; for whatever the Father does, these things the Son also does in like manner." So we see Jesus constantly watching the Father, constantly tuning in to the inner promptings of the Spirit. He doesn't ask God to bless His own agenda; instead He watches for what God is already doing and then steps in to participate. And it's no different for us now.

Let me say that again: our job is to watch for what God is doing…and participate in that.

Once Jesus is baptized in the Spirit His journey is one long chain of guidance and empowerment by the Spirit. Take a look…

- "Then Jesus was led up by the Spirit into the wilderness…" (Matthew 4:1).

- "But if I cast out demons by the Spirit of God, then the kingdom of God has come upon you" (Matthew 12:28).

- "Immediately Jesus, aware in His spirit that they were reasoning that way within themselves, said to them..." (Mark 2:8).

- "And Jesus returned to Galilee in the power of the Spirit" (Luke 4:14).

- "At that very time He rejoiced greatly in the Holy Spirit, and said, "I praise You, O Father, Lord of heaven and earth, that You have hidden these things from the wise and intelligent and have revealed them to infants" (Luke 10:21).

In passages like these we get insight into how the Spirit of God likes to work within us: The Spirit likes to guide us geographically. The Spirit likes to set people free from oppression. The Spirit likes to warn us and instruct us. The Spirit likes to equip us for miracles. The Spirit is the source of great joy in our lives. Later we see the disciples moving in the very same way as Jesus did—by the Spirit...

- "When they arrest you and hand you over, do not worry beforehand about what you are to say, but say whatever is given you in that hour; for it is not you who speak, *but it is the Holy Spirit*" (Mark 13:11).

- "Then *the Spirit said* to Philip, "Go up and join this chariot" (Acts 8:29).

- "While they were ministering to the Lord and fasting, *the Holy Spirit said*, 'Set apart for Me Barnabas and Saul for the work to which I have called them'" (Acts 13:2).

- "They passed through the Phrygian and Galatian region, having been *forbidden by the Holy Spirit* to speak the word in Asia" (Acts 16:6).

- "After looking up the disciples, we stayed there seven days; and they kept telling Paul *through the Spirit* not to set foot in Jerusalem" (Acts 21:4).

The early church seems to have been saturated with the language and operation of the Spirit, initiated at Pentecost and running rampant through the entire book of Acts. We'll see even more of this shortly.

But this operation of the Spirit was not just for the apostles. It's a free gift for every Christ-follower as Jesus affirms in Luke 11:13, "If you then, being evil, know how to give good gifts to your children, how much more will your heavenly Father give the Holy Spirit to those who ask Him?" The Father waits to be asked!

May I invite you to pause just a moment, put this book down, and ask the Father to give you more of the Holy Spirit. Ask Him to fill you up more and more until you too are hearing the

Spirit's voice and moving in the confidence and power Jesus so greatly desired us to have.

Next we're going to look at how God poured out the Spirit on those early believers and empowered them to change their world.

Your Turn

- How does the idea of Jesus living a supernatural life *as a man rather than God* impact your vision for living in the power of the Spirit?

- How do you relate to the idea that your life could have an *Immanuel* quality to it—an expression of "God with us"?

- How have you experienced the dependency on God that Jesus described as "doing nothing of Himself"?

2. FIRED UP!
Whetting Your Appetite for the Power of God

The contrast was stunning! On resurrection morning Jesus materialized inside a locked room where the disciples were huddled in fear, terrified of being discovered by either the Romans or the Temple guard. A month and a half later, they are preaching loudly and confrontationally on the streets of Jerusalem, generating both mass conversions and a storm of persecution.

With this kind of boldness Peter and John laid it on the line with the Jewish rulers: "Whether it is right in the sight of God to give heed to you rather than to God, you be the judge; for we cannot stop speaking what we have seen and heard" (Acts 4:19-20). *So what changed?* What could possibly have turned these men and women 180 degrees from cowardly to courageous?

I suspect it was two things. First, seeing the risen Christ was not just the resurrection of one man but the virtual resurrection of them all! Their purpose was reborn, and death had lost the final word. This was a revival of profound proportion! But that wasn't all…

"But you shall receive power when the Holy Spirit has come upon you; and you shall be my witnesses both in Jerusalem, and in all Judea and Samaria, and even to the remotest part of the earth" (Acts 1:8). Those were the final words of Jesus to His new community. So they gathered in a large upstairs room where they talked and ate and prayed and strategized. The expectation in that room finally erupted in divine visitation that must have scared their socks off in those first moments.

You know how they say that a tornado sounds like a freight train? Well that must have been pretty close to what they heard that morning as the presence of God broke across 120 of them, igniting what appeared to be flames of fire on their heads and activating a supernatural, instantaneous crash course in global languages. Happy chaos ensued as everyone spoke with other tongues, all at the same time! "Bewildered, amazed, marveling"—these were a few of the words for it in Acts 2 until Peter finally quiets the crowd enough to speak a gospel message that sweeps 3000 into the Kingdom of God that morning. Yes, I would call that "power."

I mentioned in the last chapter that this anointing was not merely for the apostolic era. Peter made that quite clear in his impromptu sermon: "For the promise is for you and your children, and for all who are far off, as many as the Lord our God shall call to Himself," speaking directly of this new-found gift of the Spirit in Acts 2:39. That's about as far-reaching an assurance as I can imagine when it comes to the baptism of the Holy Spirit.

One more clarification may be helpful here. We remarked, back at Jesus' baptism, that this was not His regeneration...because Jesus had no need for regeneration or salvation; He is the only one who has lived a sinless life! Now here at Pentecost, we will make the point that neither was this infilling a regeneration for those early believers, as is believed in some circles.

As we see it, the disciples were regenerated (saved) in John 20:22 when the newly-resurrected Jesus "breathed on them and said to them 'Receive the Holy Spirit.'" This can be confusing because here these same men are "receiving the Holy Spirit" a couple months later. What's clear is that the breathing-experience and the freight-train-experience were substantially different; the first seems to have sealed their allegiance to Jesus as Lord while the second dramatically delivered on the "power" Jesus promised.

The Impact of Pentecost

So let's look for a moment at what happens in these first weeks and months of the church as a result of this invasion of the Spirit:

evangelism, teaching, table fellowship, prayer, miracles, communal sharing of resources, and worship (Acts 2:41-47). Not bad, I'd say. How would you like to be part of that church?

What we really see unfolding here is a whole new level of kingdom community—a higher expression of the kingdom of God than even when Jesus was present personally. To be sure, the miracles of Jesus were extraordinary, but they were done *to* people; now we see the power of Christ taking place *among* people in such a way that creates a true community of faith. Truly the old prophecies were finally coming to pass.

Let's look at one of the stories Luke tells about Paul coming into the city of Ephesus. Finding a small community of believers, his first question to them is this: "Did you receive the Holy Spirit when you believed?" (Acts 19:2) They have not, Paul learns; in fact they don't even know there is a Holy Spirit available to receive! He learns they have been water baptized as an act of repentance, so Paul leads them to be baptized in the name of Jesus and then lays hands on them to be anointed by the Spirit— a prayer answered immediately as they begin speaking in tongues and prophesying.

The Holy Spirit is a game-changer in the early church…and He's meant to be an equally central part of our experience in the modern church.

A Jesus Multiplication

This shouldn't really surprise us. Jesus spoke directly to the priority of the Spirit's operation in His discourse at the Last Supper. He told us what to expect!

Specifically, Jesus told His disciples that He would not leave them as orphans; instead, He would send another "Helper...the Holy Spirit," who would continue to teach them the things of God and help them remember all that Jesus had spoken directly to them (John 14:18, 26). I don't know about you, but I forget things all the time—even important revelations from God that have impacted my life greatly often fade from active memory until the Spirit brings them back. I'm so grateful for this part of His job description.

This impartation of the Spirit, Jesus assured them, would be even more powerful and important in their lives than His physical presence was for them (John 16:7), a promise that probably stretched their imagination even as it sometimes does ours. And Jesus went on in this conversation to describe the guiding, comforting, illuminating Presence that would soon be theirs in the person of the Holy Spirit.

So what would happen if today's church were lit on fire by the Holy Spirit? What would happen if ordinary folks began to expect God to use them, speak through them, heal through them, meet needs through them? I think we would see kingdom community emerge! I think we would experience an unprecedented fellowship and power and presence that surprises everyone…and draws hundreds and even thousands of seekers into this *new* New Testament community.

I'm ready. How about you?

Your Turn

- How would you evaluate the level of spiritual power operating in your life today?

- How would you evaluate your experience of living in the kind of kingdom community we see in the early church?

- How would you evaluate your experience with the Spirit helping you, teaching you, and bringing the words of Jesus to mind when you need them?

3. WATERED UP!
Putting Yourself in Places to Offer Living Water

Jesus didn't seem to mind breaking convention and making people socially uncomfortable. He did this regularly with the Pharisees and even with His disciples. In John 4 we get to see Jesus operate beautifully and powerfully in the gifts and guidance of the Holy Spirit. Let's watch.

In verse 4, it says that Jesus "had to pass through Samaria." Interesting language. Why did He *have* to? Certainly, none of the disciples or anyone else from their devout community felt such compunction! But Jesus "had to" do this. My guess is that He felt it absolutely necessary, by the Holy Spirit, to take this despised path. And then there was this woman...

Jesus is weary, and I can see Him sitting on the ground, leaning back against the stone enclosure of the well, catching the shade from a nearby olive tree. And a divine appointment shows up. Did He know ahead of time who He was supposed to meet? I think not. He just knew that He was supposed to be here in Samaria, and He expected God to arrange the encounters for divine purpose.

Remember, we're saying that Jesus is our model, our example for what it looks like to be filled with and led by the Spirit of God. We're daring to believe that the Holy Spirit in you and in me can and will guide us and empower us like Jesus. Can you see yourself in this story? Could this be you sitting down to rest at the campus bus stop and noticing another student walk up?

Back to the well. The Samaritan woman approaches, and Jesus engages her practically and personally. It's hard to catch her tone as she comments on how strange it is for a Jew to ask a Samaritan for a drink. Perhaps annoyed, even bitter. Certainly surprised. We don't know, but watch Jesus' reply.

"If you knew the gift of God and who it is who says to you, 'Give me a drink,' you would have asked Him, and He would have given you living water" (v. 10). Basically, Jesus goes big here—declaring that He has the power to give her lifelong satisfaction. It's a supernatural claim, and the scope isn't lost on her. Either this traveler is full of Himself, or He's the most interesting stranger she's met in a long time. Notice too how Jesus uses her language, the vocabulary of what's right in front of them: water in a well.

If this conversation were to happen at the campus bus stop shelter, the reference might be to the bench (if you're tired) or the awning overhead (if it were raining). But it's an intersection between the natural world and the supernatural in a way that speaks to a felt need. Like being thirsty. Let's see where the woman goes next.

There's a bit of repartee as she pokes at the credibility of His claim, and He ups the ante by declaring that there is "living water" available to her that will satisfy her thirst forever! She bites: "Sir, give me this water, so I will not be thirsty, nor come all the way here to draw" (v. 15). She's still placing this conversation in the natural realm; she's either unable or unwilling to make the larger connection at this point. *Okay*, she says, *where is it?*

Gifts to Open the Heart

But before He's ready to lay out His cards, He wants to test her heart and her character. *Go call your husband*, He says. And she passes the honesty test: "I have no husband." And now Jesus tips His hand by going prophetic. "You have well said, 'I have no husband'; for you have had five husbands, and the one whom you now have is not your husband" (v. 17,18).

That catches her attention! And this really is the point of the gifts of the Spirit—to introduce a larger Presence into the conversation. To let people know that a much larger Story is at work in this simple meeting and casual conversation. There is a Source of greater knowledge and greater compassion at work—right here and right now!—than most people have imagined. And this is the beginning of Good News!

Jesus moves in the gift of prophecy by knowing which question to ask…and then in a "word of knowledge" by knowing and saying what was impossible for Him to know and say. Paul makes a point in 1 Corinthians 14:1 to prioritize the gift of prophecy. It's almost as if prophecy, or the spiritual sensitivity behind it, is the gateway to the other spiritual gifts. Said another way, the gift of prophecy is what allows people to tap into the right spiritual gift for the right occasion.

Back to our story. *Now it's the Samaritan woman's turn to test Jesus' motivations.* The woman raises the cultural issue that divides their communities to see if He is bound to His culture. And Jesus passes her test by demonstrating His allegiance to a higher culture, one far above His racial origins. He speaks with spiritual authority, and she recognizes it.

So now we're at the crux. What hangs in the balance is her heart. *Does she want it?* Is she thirsty for living water? Is her heart hungry for God? And the answer, mercifully, is yes! She is waiting for the Messiah. She is a seeker of the Christ. She longs for God to break into her world. And guess what? He just has!

And so God wants to break into the lives of many hungry souls in your world, whether it's on a campus or in a company or in a neighborhood. Messiah has come! Messiah lives in you and seeks to gather many to Himself through your heart, your hands, your words.

Your Mission, Should You Choose to Accept It

The takeaways in this inspiring encounter between Jesus and a thirsty woman are many. First, we need to be attentive to where God wants to position us. For where we're meant to live and work...and then where we're meant to go and hang out. Often there is an entire community that God draws your attention toward, whether it's poor or affluent, whether it's an organization or a health club, whether it's skaters or single moms.

Second, Jesus later instructed His disciples to look for a "person of peace" (Luke 10:6) when they launched out to spread the Good News. And here in Samaria He modeled that same strategy—finding someone open to the gospel who in turn would open doors in the community. A gatekeeper to that particular population.

So your mission field can exist on several levels: 1) the city where you are called to live, 2) the sub-community your heart is drawn to, and 3) a specific location on any given day—a place where the Spirit of God may be leading you for a divine appointment. But none of this appears until we actually believe and expect the Spirit to move us. To empower us. To water the thirsty through us. That's the catch…and the invitation.

In the wake of this woman's response to Jesus (she goes into the city as the first evangelist for the Messiah!) He then turns to His disciples for a teachable moment: *Don't say that there are still four more months until the harvest! The harvest is now. People are ready to respond to the living water now…if you'll just show up in the Spirit* (my paraphrase of John 4:35-38).

Don't say after college, after I get a job, after I get married, after I have children, after my retirement is secure… No, the kingdom is near now. People are desperate for love and salvation now. The Spirit within you is yearning to reach people right now. And it's really, really fun when we cooperate with God.

Are you ready?

Fortunately, Jesus did not leave us empty-handed. Let's look next at the tools He's given us in our mission to love and serve people by the Spirit.

Your Turn

- How does Jesus' Spirit-led encounter with the Samaritan woman speak to your life today?

- What community or sub-culture might God be drawing your heart after in a unique way?

- How might you put yourself around "wells" of opportunity?

4. TOOLED UP!
Getting Equipped with the Gifts of the Spirit

The Holy Spirit inspired connection that Jesus had with the Samaritan woman at the well apparently bore good fruit because not long after, Philip is preaching the gospel and there is a tremendous response among what I believe was the very same Samaritan community—perhaps many of whom had heard the woman's proclamations about Jesus and His living water! As crowds gather around Philip, the "power gifts" of the Spirit are in full force with healings and demonic deliverances everywhere (Acts 8:5-8).

When this good report gets back to the apostles in Jerusalem, they send Peter and John down as reinforcements and the three of them begin leading these new believers into the fullness of the Holy Spirit, laying hands on them for this new baptism of power. The signs and wonders that follow are so dramatic that a local magician named Simon is brought to faith in Christ but then gets caught in an ego-trap, offering to buy the power of the Spirit (Acts 8:9-24). Which brings a prompt rebuke from Peter! But the flow of the Spirit is in great evidence.

In this Spirit-charged environment, Philip feels a leading in his spirit. *Go to the road toward Gaza*. He doesn't know why God is sending him there, but he knows there is a divine purpose in it and has learned to discern and respond to these God-prompts with expectancy. As he is walking this road, "The Spirit said to Philip, 'Go up and join this chariot.' Philip ran up and heard him reading Isaiah the prophet, and said, 'Do you understand what you are reading?'" (Acts 8:29-30)

The man was an Ethiopian official in the queen's court who has come to worship in Jerusalem, so apparently he already has some sort of allegiance to the God of the Jews. He is a man of spiritual hunger, primed to become a follower of Jesus—just the sort of people we're wanting to be sensitive to in our own journeys. Well, the Spirit has orchestrated this supernatural meeting, and the official welcomes Philip into the chariot to help him understand Isaiah's prophecy concerning Jesus' death and atonement.

The Ethiopian is so impacted by the prophetic fulfillment of Jesus that as the chariot passes a body of water, he urges Philip to baptize him on the spot as a manifestation of his response to the gospel invitation. It is a holy moment…and a prime example of how God wants to work through His people in today's world, just as He did then.

Right Place, Right Time

So let's unpack this sequence together. First, Philip is a disciple marked as a man "full of the Spirit (Acts 6:30), so apparently, he has cultivated a sensitivity to the inner voice of God as a lifestyle. And that's where this all begins: with an immersion into the Spirit and then a life of ongoing yieldedness to the Spirit's voice.

With that as a spiritual skillset, Philip is prompted to show up in various places, ready for spiritual action—first in Samaria and then on this desert road to Gaza. Responding to the inner prompt, his spiritual radar is up, looking for divine appointments…and God does not disappoint.

Philip recognizes the Spirit's invitation to approach the Ethiopian and reaches for the "natural in," a situationally relevant point of connection—the Bible he is reading. And instead of forcing himself on the guy or preaching "hellfire and damnation," he simply asks a non-threatening question: *Do you understand what you're reading?* If the guy wasn't spiritually hungry and had not already been prepped for this very occasion, he might have said, "Huh? Oh, yeah, I got it. Thanks anyway." And I could imagine Philip saying, "Great. Have a good trip," and then looking for the next divine appointment.

Here's the thing. Reading these inspiring stories of the early church heroes, it's easy to get distracted by the sheer volume of the supernatural—angels and visions and blind eyes opening and people getting "snatched away" and disappearing—and begin to relate to these early believers as spiritual supermen, like we relate to stories about Hercules or Odysseus. And that would be to miss the point, the point of this entire book: that the same Holy Spirit who empowered Jesus and Paul and Peter and Philip is the Spirit who wants to empower you and me.

We are being invited to live every day in the ordinary extraordinariness of the kingdom of God. People surround us who are as primed to respond to the Jesus in you as the woman at the well and the Ethiopian official. Hungry. Desperate to be found by God. And for that, God has equipped us with the gifts of the Spirit. Let's take a look.

Gearing Up

1 Corinthians 12 directs us to nine tools for living the supernatural life; Paul says that "to each one is given the manifestation of the Spirit for the common good" (1 Corinthians 12:7). Not just to the spiritual elite—but to each one of us! Here's the list:

- Word of wisdom
- Word of knowledge
- Faith
- Gifts of healing
- Miracles
- Prophecy
- Discerning of spirits
- Kinds of tongues
- Interpretation of tongues

We see all of these at work in the early church, and we see all of them at work in today's church as well...or at least in churches that welcome the gifts of the Spirit. Maybe you have already seen one or two of these spiritual tools show up in your own life! An unexplainable knowing of something about another person (word of knowledge). Perhaps an ease in believing God to show up and do great things in your life (faith). Or maybe you experience an unusual number of answers when you pray for the sick (healing). The Holy Spirit is just itching to work through you!

Let's dig down a little more on the gifts themselves. The *word of wisdom* is easiest to understand in contrast with the *word of knowledge*. Where supernatural knowledge consists of divine revelation of fact (like a specific illness or injury in someone, or an event in someone's life), supernatural wisdom is knowing what to do in a situation (God wants you to take that job, or you're not supposed to buy that house right now). We saw both of these gifts illustrated in Jesus' encounter with the woman at the well.

Another example is Stephen, confronted by a crowd of Jewish scholars: "But they were unable to cope with the wisdom and the Spirit with which he was speaking" (Acts 6:10). Such is the gift that the Spirit makes available to many today.

The gift of *faith* is an intense ability to trust God to be God—to expect Him to intervene to fulfill His word and will in the world. It's a holy knowing that the goodness of God will be displayed in specific ways in specific situations. Think about Philip's obedience to follow the Spirit's direction to the desert road; my guess is that God's assignment activated the gift of faith in him: a divine expectancy that God would show up and touch lives through him that day.

Healing and *miracles* point to very specific applications of faith for God's power to be demonstrated in physical bodies and in the physical world. These gifts were prevalent throughout the early church; the chapters of the book of Acts are replete with the manifestations of these gifts. And they continue across the world today—commonplace in primitive countries (where the supernatural is expected) and filtering through into the western world despite our modern skepticism.

The gift of *prophecy* is similar to a word of knowledge in that it begins with a divine revelation of things unknown in the natural—but then moves beyond fact to application. In other words a prophetic word speaks of God's heart toward the matter revealed, specifically for the purpose of "edification, exhortation, and consolation" (1 Corinthians 14:3) in the lives of God's people.

This description indicates a shift in the New Testament application of prophecy from the Old Testament where prophesy was more of a foretelling of events to come...although we do see the prophet Agabus warning Paul that imprisonment awaited him if he continued his path to Jerusalem. More frequently in the newly formed church, prophecy is seen as a ministry tool to the people of God rather than either predictive or corrective.

The *discerning of Spirits* is a supernatural gift to see past the natural motivations and dynamics of a situation into the spiritual dimension, unveiling its origins as either God-directed, humanly engineered, or demonically derived.

Finally, the "gift" of *Tongues* needs to be distinguished from the manifestation of tongues as an indication of the Spirit's presence—what Paul describes in 1 Corinthians 14:14 as a prayer language that engages your spirit but leaves your mind out of the conversation. Praying in tongues seems to give the Holy Spirit within us a way to intercede for us directly to God.

This intercessory quality of tongues is what Paul describes in 1 Corinthians 14 as "edifying ourselves" (v. 4)—not a bad thing, as Paul assures his readers that he speaks in tongues more than anyone (v. 18)—but limited in terms of its benefit to the church at large. In order to edify and encourage the larger community, he advises them to either prophesy for the understanding of everyone...or to ask God for the *Interpretation of Tongues*, the last gift in this list.

So as it relates to speaking in tongues, it seems that there is personal prayer in tongues in the language of the Spirit that we do not understand rationally, a language that comes out of the overflow of the Spirit's presence and intercedes powerfully and personally. And then there is the gift of tongues, which is essentially a prophetic word for the Body of Christ in an unknown language that is meant to be followed by interpretation into a known language for the encouragement of the community.

Honing Your Spiritual Senses

All of these gifts of the Spirit are meant to facilitate the church in being the Body of Christ, each person a "member" of the Body and each member dependent upon the other members. "For by one Spirit we were baptized into one body...for the body is not one member, but many" (1 Corinthians 12:13,14). It's only when everyone in the church is flowing in a unique expression of the Holy Spirit that the entire community prospers and that the community grows numerically.

How do you recognize one of these supernatural gifts trying to emerge within you? It's a matter of training our spiritual senses to discern the presence of God stirring within. Like our physical senses of sight, hearing, and touch, we are always cultivating the ability to perceive spiritual dynamics—learning to "see" things with spiritual eyes...or "hear" the voice of God on the inside...or "feel" the Spirit's movement in the moment. We learn by trial and error, by practicing in safe places with seasoned spiritual leaders there to coach us. Over time our senses sharpen and the gifts become more acute.

If you are a follower of Jesus, then the Spirit of God has already taken up residence inside you...and is chomping at the bit to break out in and through you. That's why you've probably already seen hints of these gifts showing up in ways you didn't yet know how to name. But the Spirit wants to "baptize" you, to immerse you, soak you, saturate you with the very Spirit that Jesus carried. This outpouring has many benefits, some of which we've already alluded to, but primary among them is power. Power for living and moving in the kingdom of God and drawing others into that divine life.

Just one more point I'd like to make here. It seems that in the early church, leaders took every opportunity to lay hands on one another as a conduit for the Spirit's operation. In the book of Acts we see the apostles laying their hands on people for the infilling of the Spirit (8:17; 19:6), for healing and various kinds of miracles (9:12,17; 14:3; 19:11), and for commissioning others into service (13:3). So here in today's church, why settle for anything less?

Let's talk next about how to cultivate the Spirit's operation in our daily lives.

Your Turn

- If your heart is stirred to live more fully in the Spirit and to "desire earnestly [the] spiritual gifts" (1 Corinthians 14:1), ask God to baptize you afresh.

- Then ask Him which spiritual gifts He has given you and expect that He will release them more fully through you.

- Invite others in your faith community to agree with you for this new release of the Spirit's flow in your life…and then practice your new gifts within the safety and guidance of your community's leadership.

5. PAIRED UP!
Practicing the Life of the Spirit Together

The Christian life is not a solo sport! As we saw in the last chapter, the gifts of the Spirit are distributed across the church in such a way that we are dependent on one another. Can't get away from it, even in our American independence: we need each other. Spiritual isolation is a recipe for disillusionment and disempowerment, while a healthy spiritual community allows us to grow and prosper. Drift or thrive…which one sounds good to you?

In a similar way an initial baptism into the Spirit is never meant to substitute for an ongoing, sustaining core of daily and weekly spiritual practices that keep us dialed into the life and power of God. Let's look at one scene from the early church to watch how this played out in a community called Antioch. Here's how it reads…

> Now there were at Antioch, in the church that was there, prophets and teachers: Barnabas, and Simeon who was called Niger, and Lucius of Cyrene, and Manaen who had been brought up with Herod the tetrarch, and Saul. While they were ministering to the Lord and fasting, the

Holy Spirit said, "Set apart for Me Barnabas and Saul for the work to which I have called them." Then, when they had fasted and prayed and laid their hands on them, they sent them away. (Acts 13:1-3)

The first thing I notice here is that there is a leadership team in place—at least five leaders, representing at least three primary leadership gifts (prophets, teachers, and the apostolic gift of Paul/Saul). This kind of leadership plurality forms a great opportunity for a healthy spiritual discernment to flow across the entire church community.

Next, these leaders are cultivating the flow of the Spirit by engaging solid spiritual practices; in this case they are "ministering to the Lord and fasting" (v. 2). There are lots of ways to minister to the Lord including all sorts of prayer, worship, fasting, and intercession. Ministering to God involves giving Him our priority attention—both in giving and receiving. Let's explore further.

Acts of worship and prayer (the giving side) is ideally matched by acts of silence and listening (the receiving side). In the evangelical church there is high emphasis on the first side but little emphasis on the other. The more contemplative Christian traditions offer us powerful insights into a wider array of practices that keep us engaging the life of the Spirit on the listening end: solitude, silent retreats, praying the labyrinth, and centering prayer to name just a few.

Inside and Outside

Which leads to the dual nature of the spiritual life. The life of the Spirit requires both a "hidden dimension" of personal practice as well as a "public dimension" of communal practice. In Matthew 6:6 Jesus challenges His disciples to "go into your inner room, close your door and pray to your Father who is in secret, and your Father who sees what is done in secret will reward you." Alone. Just you and God.

In the intimacy of your personal relationship with God, there can be no pretenses or performances. He sees and knows you through and through—and loves you completely. "God loves you as you are, not as you should be," the late Brennan Manning spoke famously. There is no public demonstration of faith that can substitute for the personal, and so the evangelical church has rightly emphasized this dimension. Personal devotions, quiet time, daily altar—these are all expressions to describe that personal act of encountering God alone each day.

On the other hand, Hebrews 10:24-25 urges us toward the communal side: "Let us consider how to stimulate one another to love and good deeds, not forsaking our own assembling together, as in the habit of some." So our faith also requires a larger dimension—a faith community that supports and encourages and holds us accountable beyond the personal relationship.

What do both the inside and outside facets of the spiritual walk do for us? Among other things they keep us plugged into the power! They help us maintain an active, thriving infilling of the Holy Spirit, which is God's active, thriving presence on planet earth. We've already established that we cannot live in the kingdom life or help draw others into the kingdom life without the living water of the Spirit bubbling up like a well inside us.

Refreshing, encouraging, reminding, comforting, convicting, emboldening, discerning…and that list of the Spirit's operation goes on and on! It's not optional.

Practicing the Things of the Spirit

When you first learn how to ride a bicycle as a kid, it usually takes a tough mind and some skinned knees to help you master the art of balancing and steering the contraption. Which is another way of saying that it takes practice. And what doesn't? Playing a guitar, public speaking, climbing a rock wall, writing a book—none of these abilities come all at once. Every skill there is requires repetition, failure, intermediate achievement, refinement, and regularity in order to achieve a comfortable competency. And it's no different in the things of the Spirit.

Fortunately, we have much to draw upon, both from scripture and from church history to aid our personal and corporate practice. Let's take a look at a few:

Praying the Scriptures. Known in more traditional circles as *Lectio Divina*, the act of meditating upon and personalizing scripture in prayer is a powerful way to cultivate our spiritual senses. Far from a strictly mental comprehension of the biblical passage, this practice asks us to listen to the Spirit's voice in the written words—to hear God speaking to us personally and then respond to those words in faith and obedience.

Take a very short passage for this, perhaps three to five verses. Read it slowly and aloud and hold the words in silence for several minutes. Ask yourself what word or phrase stood out and caught your attention. Ask God what He wants you to do with that idea, what His invitation is to you in it. Now read the passage a second time and again, hold the words in silent expectation. Fashion God's invitation into a simple prayer where you say yes to His heart for you.

Speaking in Tongues. Because this practice "forces" your mental processes into "neutral," it is a very keen activation of the spiritual dimension of your life. It reminds us of the truth that "He who searches the hearts knows what the mind of the Spirit is, because He intercedes for the saints according to the will of God" (Romans 8:27). It reinforces our dependency upon the presence and power of the Spirit in every situation.

If you haven't spoken in tongues before, simply ask God to baptize you in His Spirit. If you know others who have received their prayer language, ask them to pray for you and with you. Surrender your voice to God and be willing to feel foolish, allowing words to come out of your mouth that you don't understand.

When it comes to speaking in tongues, there is a God-part and a you-part. When it says that "they were all filled with the Holy Spirit" in Acts 2:4, that verb is passive. They *were* filled; in other words, God did the filling. And the verse goes on to say that "they began to speak with other tongues." This is the active part: *they* spoke! You don't have to force it, but you do have to participate. Once it comes, include it as part of your regular spiritual practice.

Spiritual Journaling. Journaling is powerful in that it requires *us* to stop doing...and to reflect on what *God* is doing. It's not a diary in the sense of recording life events as much as it's a praying and processing through the spiritual events of our lives. It's a chance to pause and reflect on the spiritual meaning of events and how God is speaking to us through them. It's a chance to tag emotions and invite Jesus into them.

I encourage you to purchase a notebook that will be specific to your spiritual journaling and then practice taking ten minutes or so each morning or evening to engage God around the topics of the day. Interact with your Bible reading. Write down intercessions for people you care deeply about. Write your questions to God...and maybe even, if you're feeling bold, His answers to you! It's all about cultivating your spiritual senses to discern the heart and mind of the Spirit.

Group Discernment. Every one of us regularly comes to life intersections where we need discernment. We pray about these; occasionally we ask others to pray for us; but rarely do we invite a few trusted spiritual friends into the very act of discernment itself. And this too is a spiritual practice that yields wonderful results, both in the discernment itself and in the life of the spiritual community.

The next time you need to make an important decision—such as taking a job, moving to a new city, getting engaged for marriage, buying a house, etc.—invite your spiritual group to gather and listen for the Spirit's direction. Just like the group did at Antioch! Discuss, worship, pray, listen. Make room for the Holy Spirit to give voice to His intentions and see what happens. I'm guessing that discernment will make itself known in a clear, compelling way.

In the attentive space they created in Antioch, the word of the Lord showed up powerfully for this leadership community. The Spirit identified a new mission (which we find out about later in the chapter) and identified who was supposed to go on that mission—Barnabas and Saul. There was also an implication that they were responding to a God-inspired timetable. What a beautiful example of practicing the life of the Spirit in community.

Your Turn

- Concerning your spiritual practices, are you stronger on the personal side or the community side?

- What can you do to lean more intentionally into your weak side?

- What point of discernment do you need in your life right now…and who can you invite into the discernment process with you?

WRAP-UP

Luke, the author of the book of Acts, introduces us to an Italian soldier named Cornelius in chapter 10…and then describes how God sweeps Peter into a divinely inspired pre-lunch nap. A "trance," Luke calls it, where God provokes him to eat all sorts of animals considered unclean and forbidden by Jewish law. "Absolutely not, Lord!" Peter replies in his dream. "I have never eaten anything unholy and unclean" (v. 14). But God's reply shocks him to the core: "What God has cleansed, no longer consider unholy" (v. 15). Ah, God is changing the rules!

This scene replays three times before Peter awakens, shaken deeply by the encounter. While he's trying to sort it out, three men come calling who have been sent to invite him to meet with Cornelius and his extended family. Although Peter has yet to connect the dots intellectually, he knows enough to discern the Spirit's presence and prompting, so he goes with the men.

Eventually, God uses this event to communicate His intent, both to Peter and to the larger church, to bring gentiles into the faith community. It's a major shift in their understanding and mission…and none of it would have transpired without a complete reliance upon the operation of the Holy Spirit. Remember, this is the power source.

Just as Jesus predicted, the Spirit proved His role as the "Spirit of truth," the "Helper," and the "Counselor" (John 14). Where do you need that role in your life? Is it time to activate the life and power of the Spirit in your world?

The disciples who rocked their world with miracles and salvations were not impressive people! "Uneducated and untrained men" was the observation of the Jewish leaders. But they had one thing going for them: they were recognized as "having been with Jesus" (Acts 4:13). In other words, the Spirit of Jesus was upon them, working in them and through them. And that changed everything.

Courage, wisdom, compassion, and authority—all these things and more flow through the men and women who carry the life of the Spirit. And they will flow through you as you cultivate the work of the Spirit in your life. You will carry the grace that Jesus Himself carried because He is our model. He was our example, our model of what we are engineered to be and do. Can you believe that? Can you see yourself carrying on the same work that He began so long ago? I hope so because this is our destiny. Nothing less.

And just in case we were in any doubt, let me repeat the words I quoted in the Introduction: "Truly, truly, I say to you, he who believes in Me, the works that I do, he will do also; and greater works than these he will do; because I go to the Father" (John 14:12). That was Jesus vision for us, and you are the answer to His prayer.

As we bring this in for a landing, let's recap the big ideas from this small book.

- Jesus operated in the supernatural as a Spirit-filled human, having laid aside His divine characteristics.

- Because of that reality, we can expect to flow in the supernatural gifts of the Spirit in our sphere of influence too.

- The Holy Spirit wants to fill us up with living water and equip us with the tools we need to love people into the kingdom life of God.

- We have many great practices to incorporate into our daily lives that will keep us well connected with the life and power of the Spirit.

- And finally, the life of the Spirit is meant to be lived in community with our brothers and sisters in Christ.

So what are you waiting for? Let's follow Jesus into this grand adventure together.

ABOUT THE AUTHOR

 Jerry Daley is a veteran in church planting, having spearheaded six different church plants across North Carolina and South Carolina over those years. After serving as a Captain in the US Air Force from 1964 to 1969, Jerry was called into ministry and studied at Fuller Seminary, Golden Gate Theological Seminary, and Columbia Seminary, completing the coursework (but not the dissertation) for a D.Min. in 2013.

Jerry currently coaches, mentors, and trains pastoral leaders and teams through Game On Coaching (www.gameoncoach.com). If you are interested in having Jerry work with you or your team, he may be contacted through the website.

Jerry and his wife Nan have three grown children and eight grandchildren and reside in the mountains of North Carolina. His interests include physical fitness, reading, and endurance sports.

Made in the USA
Columbia, SC
19 August 2021

42960436R00037